CHAPTER

CW01456823

IN April 1934 Trealaw housew
Bennett gave birth to a baby
seventh child.

The baby was named Albert John and he had
brothers and sisters named Franklyn Sidney,
Marjorie Doreen, Vera, Jesse Maud, Temperance
and Edna May.

Although it was a happy time for Jesse and her
husband Albert another mouth to feed meant
more of a struggle for the family who were already
finding it difficult to make ends meet.

Jesse was the only child of her Bermuda born
father named Robert Hamilton who had managed
to get a job taking a doctor in a pony and trap
while visiting patients on the island.

On one occasion while doing the patients' rounds
the pony collided with a young child.

Frightened of what the consequences might be a
panic stricken Robert went into hiding.

After lying low for a time he ran away and became
a stowaway on a ship.

The ship eventually docked in England and he decided to settle in Devon where he found a job as a stable hand.

He proved to be a good worker and became well liked by the stable owners while he also took a shine to their daughter.

The stable owners didn't take too kindly to the relationship and despite forbidding them to continue with the relationship the young couple decided to elope and eventually set up home in Cardiff.

Cardiff would not be their permanent home however because they made the decision to move their growing family and set up home in Trealaw in the Rhondda Valley.

Times were tough in the Rhondda Valley in the 1930s with rife unemployment while there was an ongoing power struggle between the valley miners and colliery owners.

The 1930s also saw young Rhondda men board valley trains and under a cloak of secrecy head for Spain.

They were members of the International Brigade, known as Freedom Fighters, committed to help the Spanish peasants battle against the mighty armies of General Franco in what would go down in history as the Spanish Civil War.

Meanwhile the Bennett family may have been short of money but there was no shortage of music and laughter in their Trealaw household.

Jesse, who was of mixed race with her father having lived in Bermuda and Sidney, who was originally from Bristol, both loved playing the guitar along with their son Frank.

Jesse also had a wonderful singing voice as did her sister Doreen.

It seemed that Edna, the other sister, was the only one who didn't have a singing voice.

A few doors from the Bennett family was a confectionery shop owned by the Sterlini family.

In the Rhondda of those days supermarkets were very much a thing of the future.

The corner shops were always busy back then with people calling in them for a bottle of pop or a packet of fags. Just small items like that.

Corner shops were very popular with valley people and very much part of the community.

Mrs Sterlini had two sons named Aldo and Bruno and both families became very friendly and got on very well.

They were very close neighbours to the Bennett family and Mrs Sterlini took a great shine to baby John.

The Sterlinis could see that Jesse and Sidney were struggling to feed and clothe their seven children so they offered to help them out by taking John in as part of their family for a couple of months until the Bennett family could get back on their feet.

The bond between the Sterlinis and toddler John became so strong that that when the time came for John to be reunited with his family Mr and Mrs Sterlini didn't want to let him go back home.

Although Albert and Jesse were hugely grateful to Mr and Mrs Sterlini matters began to improve financially for them and they felt it was time for young John to be reunited with his family.

And so they decided to suddenly pack up their belongings and move across the valley to set up home in Weston Terrace, Edmondstown.

In those days it was what valley folk would more or less a call moonlight flit.

On the spur of the moment they just packed up and left.

It may have been just a short distance across the valley but It was the start of a new life for them.

Meanwhile the school years in Edmondstown were not a happy time for young John Bennett.

He had to quickly learn to look after himself because he was often the target of bullies.

Young John seemed to stand out from the other kids because of his darker skin and curly hair and he was often targeted in the playground.

However he was not going to allow the schoolyard bullies to get the better of him.

He wouldn't take any messing and would never back down from a schoolyard fight.

Although he wasn't an aggressive boy he never took a step back in a fight.

He had a lot to contend with back in those schoolboy days.

He had to be able to stand up for himself and because of that he gained a bit of a reputation which he didn't really want.

After leaving school John soon found a weekend job with Jack Griffiths who owned a fruit round. Like corner shops, fruit rounds were also popular back in the 1940s and 1950s.

Valley people would rely on regular visits from Jack Griffiths and his popular fruit round.

Although he wasn't earning a lot of money young John was more than eager to do the job because it helped to pay the family's bills and that was important for him.

Even back then John always knew that not only was he part of a musical family he had a good singing voice.

There used to be Sundays when the Bennett household regularly used to be packed with artistes rehearsing for concert bookings they would be scheduled to perform in.

This wasn't music to Johnny's ears however.

He just couldn't handle these occasions and used to make sure he got as far away from the house as he could.

The 1950s was an age of Teddy Boys and Rock n' Roll while Rhondda cinemas were showing Tonypandy born actor Glyn Houston, who sadly died in 2019, making his film debut in "The Blue Lamp" which also starred Meredith Edwards and Cardiff born Tessie O'Shea.

Meanwhile Ferndale born actor Stanley Baker along with Glyn Houston's brother Donald were making a name for themselves in the film industry.

Baker, who sadly died in Spain in June 1976, aged 48, starred in 1950s films as "The Cruel Sea", "The Red Beret" and "Hell Below Zero" among others.

Tonypandy born Donald Houston, who died in Portugal in 1991 at the age of 67, starred in "The Blue Lagoon" and a Welsh comedy called "A Run for your Money".

The film's story line was about Welsh coal miners David 'Dai Number 9' Jones (Donald Houston) and Thomas 'Twm' Jones (Meredith Edwards), who win a contest run by a newspaper.

The film also starred renowned actor Alec Guiness.

The prize is £100 each, plus the best seats for an important rugby union match between England and Wales at Twickenham

For the naive Welshmen, this is their first trip to England and what happened during the trip turned out to be an hilarious comedy.

While later in his career Donald Houston was cast in military roles and in comedies such as the popular "Doctor" and "Carry On" film series.

The village of Trealaw had their own rising star in a young actor called Ray Smith.

Although born in Trealaw Ray Smith lived for most of his adult life in Dinas Powys.

He became interested in acting while he was at school, and was determined not to become a miner like his father, who had been killed in a pit accident when Smith was only three years old.

After leaving school Smith became a builder's labourer.

Following National Service in the army, he began acting professionally at the Prince of Wales Theatre in Cardiff, then joined the Swansea Grand Theatre as an assistant stage manager.

He later moved to London, where he spent a year unemployed before he landed a part in a play about the Hungarian uprising.

Smith made his television debut in a programme called "Shadows of Heroes" in 1959.

Then followed this with appearances in series such as "Z-Cars" and "A Family at War" which made him known to the public.

He also appeared as Detective Inspector Percy Firbank in "Public Eye", a role he started playing in 1971.

Another role he was the tough-talking police chief Detective Superintendent Gordon Spikings, in the television series "Dempsey and Makepeace".

Two years later came one of his most famous roles, as George Barraclough in "Sam", one of Granada Television's drama series set in Northern England.

Ray Smith died at the age of 55.

He had been shooting one of his last scenes in the television adaptation of Kingsley Amis's novel "The Old Devils" when he was taken ill on location in Newport.

An onscreen credit dedicated the series "The Old Devils" to his memory, and his performance in it won him a posthumous Award for Best Actor in 1992

The wireless was very much the in house entertainment for valley people back in the 1950s. The BBC Light Programme broadcast popular radio comedy shows including "Educating Archie", with Peter Brough and Max Bygraves while people were glued to their radio sets eager to hear what was happening in" Mrs Dale's Diary" and "The Archers".

In the 1950s one of the major employers in the Rhondda was the Alfred Polikoff factory in Treorchy which began operating in the valley in 1939.

The factory became a substantial valley employment unit with an initial workforce of around 1,000 which eventually increased to 1,500. The Polikoff's factory was renamed Burberry and there was an outcry when there were plans to close it in 2007.

The factory had become a valley landmark.

The closure made national news with *The Guardian* newspaper reporting that Burberry was switching production of its polo shirts to Asia (China seems the likeliest site) or South America, and the 300-plus workers were to be made redundant.

With few companies in operation the closure signalled the end of manufacturing in the Rhondda Valley.

Treforest born singer Tom Jones added his voice to the campaign to keep luxury retailer Burberry open.

The singer sent a message to Rhondda based Welsh Assembly member Leighton Andrews to express his concerns over the proposed closure of the Treorchy plant which would mean the loss of 300 jobs.

Jones said: "As a local boy I know how important this factory has been to the community in the Rhondda.

"I therefore urge the Burberry management to withdraw their plans to close their Treorchy factory."

All the campaigning came to no avail however because in March 2007 the workforce of 300 walked out of the factory gates for the final time.

Meanwhile on the UK music scene among the popular singers of that decade were Jimmy Young, Lonnie Donegan and Cliff Richard.

There was also plenty of music to be heard in the Rhondda through choirs and brass bands.

On the sports front Manchester City captain and Rhondda born Roy Paul was celebrating after leading his side to victory in the 1956 FA Cup.

After lifting the trophy at Wembley Roy brought the Cup to the Rhondda and visited many valley schools with it much to the delight of the children.

To mark Roy's successful football career with Manchester City and Wales a plaque was unveiled outside his home in Smith Street, Gelli.

Sadly Roy died in 2002 and fittingly the plaque was unveiled by Roy's Rhondda born nephew Alan Curtis who enjoyed huge success playing for Wales and Swansea.

Trealaw is also the birthplace of former Wales, Treorchy, Aberavon and Pontypridd rugby player Paul Knight.

Front row forward Paul played five times for his country and also represented the Barbarians.

The former factory worker, who lives in a purposely built bungalow in Ystrad, has been battling Multiple Sclerosis for more than 20 years with the same determination he showed on a rugby field.

The valley also produced another rugby legend named Cliff Morgan from Trebanog who was not only capped 29 times for his country but was also a noted BBC sports commentator.

Valley teenagers would spend much of their leisure time playing records in a juke box in a local Italian café more popularly known as "The Bracchis".

The Bracchis were opened by men and women who moved to the South Wales Valleys as part of the industrial boom, capitalising on the coal and iron industry and the close knit communities that formed around collieries.

The Italian cafes became very much part of the Rhondda often becoming meeting places where customers could enjoy eating steamed pies and drinking mugs of coffee.

At one time there were around 60 Bracchis in the Rhondda Fach and Fawr.

During his teenage years Johnny Bennett would join his brothers and sisters when they visited dance halls in the valley.

One of his regular night's out was at the popular dancing session in the Judge's Hall in Trealaw. The impressive building known as the Judge's Hall, was originally called "The Judge William Memorial Hall" and was officially opened in July 1909 by Princess Louise and the Duke of Argyll. The building was a gift to the community by Lt Colonel Sir Rhys Williams and boasted a 1,500 capacity concert hall as well as a library and a billiard room,

While there Johnny asked a 16 year local old girl named Sonia Samuel for a dance.

Sonia, who worked in the Co-operative store in Tonypandy, said: "He asked for a dance and I took up his offer.

"At the time I thought he looked alright. To be honest I thought he had an Italian look about him."

That dance led to a courtship and the couple eventually got married in St Andrews Church in

Tonypandy in 1963 before spending their
honeymoon in Bournemouth
Sonia said:"My parents had friends who had
moved to Bournemouth to take over a boarding
house and our honeymoon there was their
wedding gift to us.
"We had a wonderful time there.".
Sonia also said she will never forget one
particular incident that happened on her wedding
day.
"On the day we were married my dad had lost his
voice so there was a bit of a problem when the
vicar asked:"Who giveth this woman?" and he
was unable to answer but we got over it
somehow".
"We often had a laugh about that."
John and Sonia started married life with Sonia's
parents Thomas and Doris in their terraced house
in Ynyscynon Road, Trealaw which was to
become their home for the remainder of their
married lives.
"We never really thought of buying our own home.
I suppose that's the way it was back then.

"You lived with your parents or you put your name down for a council house.

"There were never any problems living with my parents.

"We all got along fine. We were just one big happy family."

Their married life was complete when Sonia gave birth to a son named Karl in 1964.

John was now the proud father of a baby son and made sure he was providing for his family.

Sonia said:"John would always sing at any given opportunity no matter wherever we were.

"To be a singer was always his burning ambition it was as simple as that.

"I often believe that everyone is born with a certain talent and John's was his singing voice.

"I remember on one occasion we were listening to Adam Faith singing 'What Do You Want' on the radio when he turned to me and said:"I can sing like that".

Popular singer Adam Faith was a British teen idol, singer, actor and financial journalist.

He was one of the most charted acts of the 1960s and became the first UK artist to lodge his initial seven hits in the Top 5.

He was also one of the first UK acts to record original songs regularly.

Not only was he a singer but an actor also starring in several films as well as the popular 1970s TV series called "Budgie".

Sonia said:"Years later John also said the same whenever he heard Tom Jones singing "It's Not Usual" and "Delilah".

Johnny decided to set his sights on a job in the pit and after training with the National Coal Board started working as a collier in Coedely Colliery.

However Johnny knew an underground job was not for him so after a short while he quit.

Sonia said:"John just couldn't settle to life in the colliery so he decided that he needed to look for another job".

He was not unemployed for long however and eventually became a labourer with his brother in law Ken Griffiths who was a scaffolder back in those days.

John was still unable to settle in his working life and once again felt he needed to look elsewhere for employment.

 He eventually found one as an agent with the Ynyshir based S and U clothing company.

Sonia said:"John's job was collecting payments from people and his round was in Dinas which was difficult to say the least.

"Back then times were hard in the valley which meant that customers were sometimes shy of making payments.

"But John became popular with his customers when they realised he was Jesse Bennett's son and the payments started to come in.

"He enjoyed his job especially meeting up with people because he loved to talk.

"John definitely had the gift of the gab".

CHAPTER 2

KEN Griffiths quickly realised that Johnny had a good singing voice and he kept persuading him to put it to good use.

Sonia said:"Ken kept on urging John to perform at local drinking clubs but he didn't want to know.

"He loved nothing better than breaking into song but there was no way he was going to do so in front of an audience".

Ken wasn't giving up that easily however and gave John a bit of a shock when he told him that he had booked him a singing spot in a concert at the Tynewydd Labour Club at the top end of the Rhondda.

Sonia said:"John wasn't happy about it and said there was no way he would do it but he eventually gave in which pleased Ken."

The Tynewydd Labour Club was hugely popular in the valley with many top acts providing the entertainment there.

In its heyday the club, which was founded in 1912, had well over a thousand members.

When the club held its annual children's outing more than 40 double deckers were hired to take members and their families for a day out at the seaside.

Sadly with drinking club life in the valley on the decline the Tynewydd closed its doors for the final time in September 2015.

Sonia said:"Emrys Richards, who was a lovely character and well known throughout the valley was the compere of the Tynewydd Labour Club and although John was very nervous about going on the stage for the first time Emrys was a great help to him.

"John was always grateful for the support Emrys gave him. He never forgot that."

The popular club compere and chairman sadly died at the Royal Glamorgan hospital in 2008.

Mr Richards, who lived in Halifax Terrace, Tynewydd, before becoming a resident in Ty Pentwyn nursing home, was well known throughout the Rhondda.

A spokesman for the Tynewydd Labour Club paid tribute to Mr Richards and said: "It is a very sad day for the club.

"Emrys was a loyal servant of the club for many years and will be much missed."

Sonia said:"On his stage debut John sang three songs which went down so well with the audience that he got another booking.

"He loved every minute he was on stage and often talked about it.

He never forgot the first time he sang to an audience,

"He always had a soft spot for the Tynewydd Labour."

After that first stage performance at the Tynewydd club Johnny got the singing bug and never looked back.

Sonia said:"It didn't surprise me. John always wanted to sing and I suppose getting that response from the audience meant a lot to him.

"He had got a taste of singing on a stage in front of an audience and there was no turning back after that."

In the 1960s the Rhondda was teeming with workingmen's clubs including The Naval Club in Tonypandy, Pentre Legion, Pentre Labour the NUM Club in Tonypandy and the Lewis Merthyr club in Porth among many others.

The Rhondda Fach also had its own drinking haunts including Wattstown Social, Tylorstown Con and Pontygwaith Cosmo.

Saturday nights were the high spots of the week with club concert halls filled with swirling cigarette smoke, bingo books and busted beer mats.

It was the era of concert nights when the turns would take to the stage in front of booze filled audiences who demanded top value entertainment for much needed Saturday nights out.

Many artistes who made it big in the world of showbiz did many of their early performances in valley workingmens' clubs.

For visiting artistes the most feared man was the club's entertainment secretary.

If the club's entertainment secretary could sense that the club members did not appreciate a performer he had the power to whisper the dreaded words at the interval which were "I'm paying you off" because the act had failed to please the audience.

But Trealaw born Johnny Bennett was a singer who was "never going to be paid off."

Sonia said:"John's singing act was a mixture of ballads and beat and the audiences loved it".

The song Johnny loved to sing was "Summertime" which was composed in 1934 by George Gershwin for the 1935 opera "Porgy and Bess" and performed by Ella Fitzgerald among others.

He also loved singing "I who have Nothing" a song recorded by Cardiff born singing star Shirley Bassey among others.

Sonia said:"John loved that song, it was very close to his heart".

Although Johnny was becoming more and more popular Ken Griffiths still felt that he needed somebody to accompany him.

Sonia said:"Ken persisted in reminding John that he needed a backing group.

"I remember he was joined by a lovely girl singer from Brecon who had a wonderful voice and a local chap named Cliff Jones who could sing like Tony Bennett.

"Another singer I remember who had a really captivating voice was Gwyn Davies from Clydach Vale who eventually emigrated to Australia with his family.

"There were a lot of talented singers performing on the club stages back in those days."

John also met up with a chap called Malcolm Innocent and they formed a concert party called "The Innocents" all the while keeping busy performing in clubs throughout the valleys.

Sonia said:"John also decided to join another group called "The Spades" which was made up of Colin Mackie, Emrys Jones and Karl Roberts".

Rhondda born Colin Mackie, who has sadly passed away, was well known as a brilliant guitarist.

He played with the Nantymoel based Perkins brothers, who won the Marlborough Country and Western event at Wembley in the early 1980s.

Nantymoel resident Kevin Morgan also has fond memories of Colin Mackie.

He said:"I was once in Colin's house when a Rolls Royce pulled up outside and in walked Andy

Fairweather Low calling to get his guitar repaired".

Andy Fairweather Low was born in Ystrad Mynach and first found fame as a founding member of the pop group Amen Corner in the late 1960s.

They had four successive Top 10 hits in the UK Singles Chart, including the single If "Paradise Is Half as Nice" in 1969.

In the 1960s Colin also played in a group called "The Diamonds".

Ieuan Rees also recalls seeing Colin perform with "The Diamonds" in the Palace in Tynewydd.

Meanwhile Norman Cox remembers Colin as being a great guitar maker and he still has one of his semi acoustic Rickenbacker copies.

Rickenbacker instruments stand as some of the most iconic of all time, as one of the true early innovators of the electric guitar

Marion Evans recalls that Colin also played with Jack Bass and Rob Evans who were also in a backing group for Johnny Bennett.

Marion said that Rob along with the Perkins brothers and Colin Mackie were due to perform at a club in Nantymoel. when Colin couldn't find his guitar.

"It did look as if they would not be able to perform.

"Colin had left it outside his house and when he drove back to his home in Treherbert he found his guitar which was still on the pavement where he had left it".

Meanwhile Johnny's sister Jesse became very ill and Ken had to give up organizing gigs for the concert party to spend time looking after his wife. Sonia said:"Although Ken loved being part of John's singing career his priority was looking after his wife

"He needed to be there for her it was as simple as that."

This meant that Johnny had to stop performing for a few months although he made sure he fulfilled some bookings that Ken had made.

"John couldn't wait to get back on the stage again and of course when he sang at these bookings he was always asked to come back and perform again.

"John would never let an audience down. That wasn't his style.

Whatever happened he was determined to fulfil those bookings."

John's singing career became back on track when Sonia decided to take up running an agency for him which proved very successful.

Sonia said: "John was keen to start performing again and although it would be quite a task I didn't mind stepping in.

"His engagements were getting busier in the Rhondda and elsewhere and I was only too willing to help.

"I have wonderful memories of the times we often went to John's bookings in a van owned by family friends named Des and Mair Pugh who lived near us in Trealaw.

"I will never forget those occasions. They were lovely days, always full of fun, We were like one big happy family.".

Sonia also recalled the time when a chap visited Johnny to show him a guitar.

"It was a Dobro make guitar and a quite rare instrument I believe".

The Dobro is an actual guitar that was created by the Dopyera Brothers, one of whom was the inventor of the resonator guitar

"The chap asked John if he would like to buy it. The guitar once belonged to John's father so it had sentimental value.

"Of course John didn't hesitate he jumped at the chance to buy it.

"He wasn't going to pass it up.

"Mind you I never knew how much he paid for it because he wouldn't tell me.

" I often think about that."

Sonia was now being kept very busy taking John's bookings on the telephone in their Trealaw home.

"It was incredible the telephone never stopped ringing".

Johnny was becoming so popular that there were even people knocking the front door wanting to know where his next booking was so they could go and see him perform.

Sonia said:"It just showed how popular he had become".

He was being kept busy performing on stage and was enjoying every minute of it.

"My parents were very pleased with John's success.

"If the phone rang when I was out they would make sure they made a note of the names of the people interested in booking John so I could get back to them.

"There was never a dull moment and as time went on I got more and more busier taking bookings for John.

"It really was a very busy time for us."

It was while Johnny Bennett was become more and more in demand at valley venues that he would become pals with a Treforest born singer who would go on to become a huge star in the world of show business.

CHAPTER 3

IN the 1960s and 1970s talented vocalists were much in demand in the pubs and workingmens' clubs in the South Wales Valleys.

Rhondda born Billy Gover, who used to be called the "Welsh Bing Crosby", Martyn Lewis, Des Rees, John Gimson, Bobby Gilbert and Dai Priday along with a Trealaw born singer named Johnny Bennett were much in demand for club concert nights and "Go as you Please" events.

Rhondda resident Allan Griffiths said:"I remember Johnny singing in the Lewis Merthyr club on many occasions.

"The audiences loved him.

"He always had a great ovation whenever he performed.

"He was very popular in valley clubs.

"Billy Gover, who was my uncle,was also a very well known singer in the valley.

"He also entertained the troops so I've been told.

"Apparently Billy could have gone a lot further with his career with some of the big bands of the day including the "Black and White Minstrels" show.

The Black and White Minstrels" show featured white performers "blacked up" as minstrels and although condemned as politically incorrect it became extremely popular on BBC television in the 1950s.

The show ran for twenty years on BBC prime-time television.

Beginning in 1958, it was a weekly light entertainment and variety show which presented traditional American minstrel and country songs, as well as show tunes and music hall numbers, and with lavish costumes.

Allan said: "Billy was very much a home bird at heart and was never happier than singing in the local clubs

"He enjoyed socializing and having a few beers and he was also part of the "Rhondda Rascals" concert party.

He said: "I have wonderful memories of Billy. He was an amazing character."

With his singing mixture of Rock and Roll and ballads Johnny Bennett was becoming a regular performer on the valleys club circuit.

It was while Johnny was performing at a pub in Dinas that he met a fellow entertainer named Tommy Scott.

Treforest born Tommy Scott got an unexpected break when a local band called "The Senators" asked him to step in for regular frontman Tommy Pitman.

Tommy was initially reluctant to play the Friday night gig because the venue, the YMCA in Pontypridd, didn't serve alcohol.

The gig was such a success however that, when Tommy Pitman wanted his lead spot back, the band voted to keep Tommy Scott as their new frontman.

The Group recorded four demo tracks in the football changing rooms at Pontypridd YMCA, known as the "bathroom session".

Pontypridd YMCA was founded in 1882 by a small but dedicated group of volunteers, while the current building was opened in 1910 through public donations.

The Pontypridd landmark was also a second home for singing stars Sir Geraint Evans and

Stuart Burrows who were both born in William Street, Cilfynydd.

Sir Geraint and Stuart enjoyed success as opera singers.

In 2010 Tom Jones made a nostalgic return to the YMCA building in the heart of Pontypridd.

There was quite a shock for Pontypridd town traders and shoppers when they saw a BMW with blacked out windows pull up outside the YMCA building and Tom Jones stepping out of it.

The *Pontypridd Observer* newspaper reported that Spike Griffiths, who was an arts co-ordinator for RCT council, managed to have his picture taken with the music legend while he was running an arts workshop for young people at the YMCA. He said: "We had no idea he was coming in to be part of a film."

Hayley Fidler, the then manager of Pontypridd YMCA, said she didn't know anything about the star's visit.

Hayley said: "I knew someone was coming in to do some filming, but I was told it was going to be about the choral tradition and the next thing I know Tom Jones walks in.

"It was a complete surprise."

It was believed at the time that the singer was in the area to film a programme for American TV network CBS.

The singer also made a visit back to his hometown in 2005 to celebrate his 65th birthday. He was back in his home town to hold a special open air concert in Ynysyngharad Park in front of 25,000 fans.

The singer said that the reason why he had opted to celebrate his 65th birthday with a massive concert in his own back yard Pontypridd is simply because he wanted to perform once again in the home town where his illustrious career started.

"I spent the first 24 years of my life in Wales, so that never leaves you," he told the *Pontypridd Observer* newspaper.

"I carry Wales with me all the time. It's part of me: I'm Welsh."

Therefore due to his fierce patriotism, there was only one place where he wanted to stage his only UK concert. in Ynysangharad Park, or Ponty Park, as he affectionately calls it.

Following months of careful planning by Tom and his team, a total of 25,000 fans had the chance to see him perform at the open-air concert,

His show was planned to be similar to the ones he performed at venues across America, where he was based.

"I will come over with my band and do my 90-minute show and keep the big songs in like "Green Green Grass of Home," said Tom, who lived in Los Angeles, as details of the gig were unveiled.

The singer said at the time:"I love Ponty Park and I have a lot of wonderful memories there.

"The Park is a perfect place to bring everyone together.

"It's a beautiful spot and deserves to be playing an important part in creating many special moments in people's lives".

It proved to be a memorable night as Jones sang within a few hundred yards of his home.

The singer was greeted like a conquering hero as he appeared, dressed in lilac suit, studded black shirt and familiar cross medallion around his neck.

Naturally, his greatest hits wrought a huge ovation from the breakthrough number one "It's Not Unusual", through to "What's New Pussycat", "Thunderball", and "Delilah".

And of course "The Green, Green Grass of Home", with a nod of the head towards Laura Street as he reached the line "The old house is still standing, though the paint is cracked and dry."

In between songs, Jones fondly recalled his visits to Ponty Park as a young boy and with his own son Mark, born when Tom Woodward was a teenager dreaming of stardom.

Although he had adopted the stage name of Tommy Scott, back in the 1960s the singer was born Thomas John Woodward, and spent his younger at the family home in Kingsland Terrace, Treforest.

His parents were Thomas Woodward who was a coal miner, while Freda was his mother's name. Tom attended Wood Road Infants School, Wood Road Junior School and Pontypridd Central Secondary Modern School.

He began singing at an early age and would regularly sing at family gatherings, weddings and in his school choir.

The Treforest youngster did not like school or sports, but gained confidence through his singing talent.

At the age of 12 he was diagnosed with Tuberculosis.

Many years later the singer is quoted as saying:"I spent two years in bed recovering. It was the worst time of my life."

During convalescence he could do little else but listen to music and draw.

Sonia said:"John took a liking to Thomas Woodward, who had now changed his name to Tommy Scott, the first time he met him.They got on well together.

"He could sense he was a very talented vocalist and a big hit with club audiences".

Meanwhile Sonia recalled the first time she saw Tommy Scott performing in a local pub.

Sonia said: "I often think back to that time and always with a smile.

"To be honest I wasn't all that impressed with this singer called Tommy Scott.

"He had a broken nose, wore Teddy Boy clothes and I didn't think he was all that good looking".

Tom hated his mis-shapen nose, which had been broken many times in fights when he was a Teddy Boy.

Eventually, he persuaded his manager to let him have it fixed in an operation that was officially to 'repair some nasal cartilage'.

"I just couldn't see him making an impact in the music business.

"It just shows how wrong I was at the time."

The two singers met on several occasions and became close pals while performing in valley clubs.

There were many people who could not help but notice how much they resembled each other.

Sonia said:"It was quite strange because there was a striking resemblance between them which was rather uncanny.

"A lot of people used to comment about it."

It was during this time that Johnny also struck up a friendship with a young musician called Gordon

Mills, who would eventually become Tom Jones' manager,

London based Mills, who spent his younger years in the Rhondda, was enjoying much success as a music manager and a songwriter.

Sonia said:"Gordon Mills may have lived away from the valley but he never lost his love of the Rhondda.

"He frequently came back for a visit and would make a point of dropping by to see us.

"We were always delighted to see him."

"He loved meeting up with John and they used to spend a lot of time together"

In later years Johnny would often recall the times when Gordon used to visit him and the pair would drive down to Brithweunydd Road, Trealaw.

In an interview with *Rhondda Leader* reporter Dave Edwards in the 1980s Johnny said:"Myself and Gordon would for a long while just sit in his car parked opposite the house where he spent his younger years.

"I would urge Gordon to go and knock the door because I am certain the people who were living there would have invited him in.

"But Gordon was having none of it.

"I could see the house held a lot of memories for him but he didn't want to go inside. It was quite sad really.

"He just wanted to sit in the car and stare at the house.

"I could never understand why. I suppose there must have been a reason but I could never figure it out.

"Then after a while he would say: 'Come on Johnny let's go over to a Tonypandy cafe and get some pie and chips'".

"He loved eating in a valley café it was something I think he missed.

"I suppose it was something he did quite often while growing up in the Rhondda."

It was on one of these visits that Johnny happened to mention Tommy Scott to Gordon Mills who didn't show a lot of interest.

Although reluctant to meet up with the singer Johnny persuaded Mills to watch Tommy and the Senators perform at the Lewis Merthyr Club in Porth on a Sunday morning before he travelled back to London.

Tommy didn't have any transport so John drove to his home in Treforest to pick him up.

When Mills arrived at the Porth Club he said to Johnny:"Where's this guy Tommy Scott?"

Johnny nodded towards the Treforest born singer who was sitting a few tables away and he could see that Mills wasn't impressed by what he saw.

Sonia said:"Gordon just wasn't bothered.

"We were all shocked when Gordon said he wasn't interested.

"John was quite taken aback and couldn't understand it"

Johnny didn't give up however and again he was able to persuade a reluctant Gordon Mills to visit the Top Hat Club in Cwmtillery in 1964 where Tommy Scott and his group "The Senators" were performing.

Former model and showgirl Mandy Rice-Davies, who gained notoriety with her links to the John Profumo affair, was also booked to be guest at the event but was forced to cry off because of laryngitis.

Born in Llanelli Marilyn Davies, known as Mandy Rice-Davies was a Welsh model and showgirl best

known for her association with Christine Keeler
and her role in the Profumo affair, which
discredited the Conservative government of
British Prime Minister Harold Macmillan in 1963.
While performing in valley clubs over the years
Johnny was well aware of the power the club
committee could wield.

He knew from experience that it didn't pay to
upset them.

If the act wasn't well received a singer's
performance would end quickly.

And that was something he would very much
encounter at the Top Hat Club all those years ago.

When he and Gordon, along with their wives Jo
and Sonia, who were both pregnant at the time,
attempted to get seats in the concert room they
were refused entry.

Sonia said:"There was no way we were being
allowed to go in. We couldn't believe it.

"Instead we were told by a committeeman to go
into the bar and remain there".

The club committee's rules were that only
members were allowed into the concert room.

An embarrassed Johnny pleaded with the committee to let them into the concert room.

Sonia said:"John had to practically beg them to let them in but they were having none of it.

"We just didn't know where to look and It became quite embarrassing.

"John kept telling the committee that Gordon Mills had travelled down from London to see Tom and the Senators perform but they didn't want to know.It was very frustrating.

"They just weren't prepared to give an inch and were determined to play it by the rules."

After a great deal of persuasion the committee eventually gave in.

But on the condition that they stayed by the door and didn't get in the way of anything,

The Senators opened with the song "I'll Never Get Over You" which was a hit for Johnny Kidd and the Pirates.

Tommy then came on stage and gave a rousing version of the song "Spanish Harlem" which went down really well with the audience.

Johnny said:"Although Tommy knocked the audience dead Mills shrugged his shoulders and said he wasn't convinced he could make it big. "We just couldn't believe it."

Mills told him "Come on Johnny let's forget it. "These groups are ten a penny.

"I'm a busy man and I need to get back home. I've had my fill of this".

But Johnny knew Mills was a crafty customer and sensed he was interested.

Johnny said:"I think it really struck home when Gordon's wife said that Tom was too big for a workingmen's club and that he belonged in the bright lights of London'."

In November 2011 the Top Hat club which was always linked to Tom Jones was destroyed by fire.

The cause of the fire was never discovered and remains a mystery.

Vernon Hopkins, the founder of the Senators group, now a singer-songwriter living in Swansea, told *WalesOnline* of his sadness that the club has been damaged beyond repair.

He said: "Our main venue was the YMCA in Pontypridd.

"But you could say that it was at the Top Hat where things really took off.

"Tom joined us in 1961 when we were playing in Pontypridd for £5 a night.

"But we would also play in the clubs across the Valleys.

"One night, out in the middle of nowhere in this club called the Top Hat in Cwmtillery, we persuaded Gordon Mills to come down and listen to us.

"It was a small club with a very small stage.

"It was a bit insignificant. I can remember it had very narrow doorways".

In an interview for *BBC Radio Wales* Tom Jones said:"We had these two managers called Myron and Byron".

Joint managers Raymond William Godfrey and Raymond John Glastonbury (Myron and Byron), had already signed the singer to Decca Records, after terminating their previous recording agreement with Joe Meek of RGM Sound Ltd.

They retained a five per cent interest in Jones, but had to sue the singer and Mills in London's High Court for non fulfillment, finally obtaining a settlement in 1969 for an undisclosed sum.

Tom Jones said:"They were both Welsh boys and they wanted to be songwriters.

"They were managing us and trying to get these songs away, you know trying to get a record contract for us.

"And then Gordon Mills showed up and it just went from there."

"He came to visit relatives in the Rhondda because that is where he spent his younger years.

"He also wanted to visit friends of ours named Johnny Bennett and Gordon Jones who grew up with Gordon Mills, they went to school with him.

"They were all good friends.

"Johnny Bennett got in touch with me and said that he would arrange for me to meet Gordon

"I was singing with the Senators in this club in Cwmtillery called "The Top Hat Club".

"It sounds very posh but it wasn't.

"While we were playing there Gordon and his wife came along and saw the show and that is how it all began".

Mills eventually signed a contract with the singer called Tommy Scott which was witnessed by Johnny Bennett.

Mills then took the young singer back to London with him and began making plans for his future.

The next time Johnny would meet Tom was in the Cymmer Pioneer club in Porth.

Johnny knew that Tom was visiting his family in Treforest and did a favour for a fan named Dorothy Hood who begged him to take her to see the singer at his Treforest home.

Sonia said: "Dorothy was a huge fan of Tom and she was over the moon when John agreed to take her to Treforest."

The singer wanted to know what Johnny was doing that night and when he told him he was booked for the Cymmer Pioneer Club he asked if he could come along with his family.

Johnny said:"The club used to be packed out in those days with mostly members and the only way I could book a table was to tell the secretary that it was for some of my family and hope for the best".

While Johnny was performing on stage an excited young boy came running down the hall and said to a committee man:"There's a man called Tom Jones waiting outside and he is not being allowed in."

Tom and his family were eventually allowed in and the Treforest born singer even went on stage and sang a few of his numbers for the audience.

Sonia said:" Tom and his family sat around a table and without much persuasion he got up on the stage and sang.

"But there was a surprise when the audience were soon calling for John to get back on the stage and sing more songs.

"It was quite a turnaround really but although he was sort of upstaged to be fair Tom took it really well."

It was during a short visit home in 1966 that Tom had some great news.

He received a telegram to say that his song "The Green, Green, Grass of Home" had reached number one in the hit parade,

It was Number One on 3rd December 1966 and stayed there for seven weeks and was the Christmas number one of this year

"The Green, Green Grass of Home", written by Claude "Curly" Putman, Jr. and first recorded by singer Johnny Darrell, is a country song originally made popular by Porter Wagoner in 1965, when it reached No. 4 on the country chart.

That same year, it was sung by Bobby Bare and by Jerry Lee Lewis, who included it his album Country Songs for City Folks.

Tom Jones learned the song from Lewis' version, and in 1966, he had a worldwide No. 1 hit with it. In the following years Mills also guided a singer called Gilbert O'Sullivan to chart success.

Gilbert O'Sullivan is an Irish-English singer-songwriter, best known for his early 1970s hits "Alone Again", "Clair", and "Get Down".

O'Sullivan enjoyed nearly five years of success with MAM, founded by Gordon Mills and Tom Jones.

His hits seven UK Top 10 singles and four UK Top 10 albums; three US Top 10 singles and one top 10 album; five Dutch Top 10 singles and three

Top 10 albums; five New Zealand Top 10 singles; three Canadian Top 10 singles; and seven Japan Top 10 singles.

O'Sullivan discovered his recording contract with MAM Records greatly favoured Gordon Mills resulting in a lawsuit focusing over how much money O'Sullivan's songs had earned and how much payment he had actually received.

In May 1982, the court found in O'Sullivan's favour, describing him as a "patently honest and decent man", who had not received a just proportion of the vast income his songs had generated.

The singer was awarded £7 million in damages.

CHAPTER 4

IT was a Saturday night and the Pentre Labour club was packed out with not an empty seat anywhere.

On stage was one of Rhondda's best known concert parties which went under the name "The Spades".

The popular valley group was very much a family affair with Madame Bennett, Sid, Frank and Doreen Bennett doing their stage act while also on stage was a tall rather brash teenager named Gordon Mills.

As always the family show proved to be a great hit and as they took their bow after another successful night young Mills revelled in the accolades.

Although born in Madras, British India Gordon Mills was brought up in the Rhondda. Mills's parents Bill and Lorna met and married in British India when his father was serving in the British Army.
They returned to Britain shortly after Gordon's birth. He was their only child.

At the age of 15 Mills left school and there followed several jobs including the steelworks, the colliery and the motor trade before he enlisted in the National Service and served in Germany and Malaya.

After finishing his National Service Mills returned home to the Rhondda and managed to get a job as a bus conductor with Rhondda Transport.

At its peak in the 1950s, Rhondda Transport was the biggest bus company in Wales with a fleet of more than 200 buses.

It was taken over by Western Welsh in 1971.

In 1956 the Rhondda Transport Company operated 207 buses, 130 of which were double-decker and the number of staff during December totalled 970.

At this time the general manager was TL Strange, and the Rhondda Transport Company would shortly become the largest operating bus company in South Wales.

With an eventual total of 217 buses, 30 had to be stabled in Cymmer Yard and eight near the company's paint shop at Abergorki in Treorchy.

Growing up in the valley Gordon struck up friendships with not only Johnny Bennett but also with Gordon Jones and Albert Blinkhorn.

While working on the buses he also got friendly with a staff member named Frankie Bennett, who was Johnny Bennett's brother.

Gordon had been given a harmonica as a present and while visiting a pal named Albert Blinkhorn he discovered his friend could play the instrument. Gordon took a great interest in that.

Ian Palmer said:" Albert Blinkhorn was my father in law.

"He went on to master several other instruments including keyboard, saxophone, clarinet and guitar.

"He played in his own and different bands in the valleys for many years.

The only other persons I can remember was Johnny Benbow a drummer also from Trealaw and Ceri who played the organ.

"In later years Albert moved to Llantrisant where he set up his own recording studio in the front room taping and mixing for local bands who were starting off.

"Albert sadly passed some years ago but the family still has most of the instruments. "In our house we have a box containing over 40 harmonicas umpteen guitars and saxes and lots of great memories."

Albert Blinkhorn's skill of harmonica playing was of great interest to Gordon who was keen to play the instrument and with the help of his mother Lorna he quickly learned how to play the harmonica

Mills soon played it well and it was the platform he would build on.

Even at that young age Mills had a keen business brain and soon became aware that he could turn his harmonica playing into a money spinner.

With that in mind he decided to join a local concert party called "The Spades" which was Johnny Bennett's mother's concert party.

The Spades proved to be a popular concert party and were never short of bookings.

"I'm going to get somewhere in life," young Mills used to brag to his valley pals,"you just wait and see".

Mills was once quoted as saying: "I would look at a nice car and think, 'I'd like that car' not because I was jealous of the man driving it or wonder why he should have it and not me.

"Same with a house.If I saw a beautiful place in the country in some magazine it would stay at the back of my mind because I always knew I wanted my own little place in the sun, as rosy as I could make it."

The teenager, entered the British Harmonica Championships which was sponsored by the renowned harmonica player Ronald Chesney

An acclaimed harmonica player Chesney along with Ronald Wolfe were the creators of the popular TV series "On the Buses" and "The Rag Trade.".

Mills did well enough to book a spot in the World Championships which was organised by the great Larry Adler.

Larry Adler, who died in 2001 was an accomplished American harmonica player.

He was well known for playing major works,

During his later career he collaborated with Sting, Elton John, Kate Bush and Welsh born singer Cerys Matthews, who was a founding member of Welsh rock band Catatonia and a leading figure in the "Cool Cymru" movement of the late 1990s.

Adler was also one of the guests at the opening of the Porth based Pop Factory in 2000.

Mills was now getting noticed in the world of variety and in the late 1950s he was given a spot in the Morton Fraser Harmonica Gang, a musical comedy act which was hugely popular on the variety circuit.

While performing with them he met Don Paul and Ronnie Wells and together they formed a trio known as "The Viscounts".

They quit the Harmonica Gang and formed "The Viscounts" in late April 1958, playing local shows and eventually attracting the attention of manager Larry Parnes who got them billed at better venues and signed them to Pye Records in 1960.
Larry Parnes was an English pop manager and impresario who was enjoying success in the world of entertainment.

He was the first major British Rock manager, and his stable of singers included many of the most successful British rock singers of the late 1950s and early 1960s.

The group's cover version of Ray Smith's hit single "Rockin' Little Angel" became a hit in Australia.

Meanwhile their cover of "Shortnin' Bread" hit number 16 in November that year in the UK Singles Chart.

In 1961 their single cover version of "Who Put the Bomp (In the Bomp, Bomp, Bomp)" reached number 21 in the UK chart, spending ten weeks in the listings.

The group toured with Gene Vincent and Eddie Cochran, as well as sharing a stage with The Beatles in 1963 opening for American singer Chris Montez.

Chris Montez is an American guitarist and vocalist, whose stylistic approach has ranged from "Rock and Roll" to pop standards and Latin music.

His rock sound is exemplified in songs such as his 1962 hit "Let's Dance".

In 1964, "The Viscounts" moved to Columbia Records, but none of their three following singles charted.

Mills eventually quit the group to become an established song writer in London.

His first hit was "I'll Never Get Over You" recorded by Johnny Kidd and the Pirates which reached Number four in the British Charts in 1963.

In the space of a year he wrote more hits, "Hungry For Love", "Three Little Words" and "I'm The Lonely One" which gave Cliff Richard a top 10 in 1964.

After putting Tom Jones and others on the path to stardom a wealthy Gordon Mills joined the Jet Set of Weybridge in Surrey where he bought a property he named "Little Rhondda".

Weybridge was a popular location for many star names.

Among the past residents there are John Lennon, Ringo Starr, Cliff Richard, Elton John and Eric Sykes.

Mills eventually moved to Los Angeles and in 1970 together with Tom Jones went on to found the MAM (Management Agency & Music Ltd).

The first single released on MAM was "I Hear You Knocking" by Dave Edmunds in 1970.

Later that year, Gilbert O'Sullivan started his run of hit singles on MAM with the song "Nothing Rhymed".

In 1986 Mills had been in hospital in Los Angeles for three weeks after complaining about stomach pains.

However what he thought would be only routine tests turned out to be far more sinister.

Doctors diagnosed stomach cancer and at the age of 51 in July 1986 Gordon Mills passed away.

Superstar Tom Jones was devastated when he heard the news.

After hearing manager to the stars was dead within a few days.of Gordon's death Tom was unable to speak for hours and went into a room alone in his house in Bel Air Los Angeles to have a good cry and reminisce about the man who was the driving power behind him.

After Gordon's death, 'It's Not Unusual" was re released and Tom Jones, found himself back at the top of the charts.

Tom's cousin Alun Woodward was a great friend of Gordon's and only recently visited America where he was feted and entertained at Gordon's house in Bel Air.

Alan said in an interview that his death had come as a great shock.

He said:"Tom and Gordon we're more like brothers than manager and singing star.

"The years they spent together brought them very close and their relationship was one of the closest in show business.

"They had their ups and downs but at the end of the day they always came to a compromise.

"Gordon was a very forceful and dominating figure as far as the business side of the relationship was concerned.

"He had the charm which he could turn to their advantage.

"He was one of the hardest negotiators for Tom's contracts all over the world.

"God threw away the mould when he made Gordon Mills.

"His passing his a huge loss not only for Tom but the but for the world of show business".

The Rhondda Civic Society paid tribute to Mills by placing a plaque on one of his former homes in Brithweunydd Road, Trealaw.

Mills was the Las Vegas regular's manager and co-songwriter and family members even said the man who has become known as "The Voice" may not have become the colossus he is today had it not been for the former bus conductor.

Mr Mills son, who is also called Gordon, is a songwriter and producer from Weybridge, Surrey and he co-wrote Newton Faulkner's hit "Dream Catch Me".

Speaking outside his dad's old house he said: "I think they would be doing pretty much what they were doing before he discovered them.

"If it was just one singer he discovered it could have been a fluke, but not for someone to have done it three times with Tom Jones, Engelbert Humperdinck and Gilbert O'Sullivan."

Mr Mills' former wife Jo, who also lived in Weybridge, was at the ceremony also.

The Rhodesian-born former Miss South Africa runner-up, who helped Mills with his songwriting, said: "Who knows where they would be?

"They were each talented but the route was far quicker having met Gordon.

"I think Tom would have made something of himself sooner or later, but I doubt it would have been by the direct route he had."

About 30 people gathered for the unveiling of the grey granite stone, which simply read: "Gordon Mills, 1935-1986 lived here.

Songwriter and manager of Tom Jones."

Since there was no actual veil, Mills' son stood in front of it until Rhondda Cynon Taff deputy mayor Rob Smith finished giving a speech.

Councillor Smith, who passed away in May 2019, said: "He was known as Mills the Man of Music and that was quite fitting."

Rhondda Borough Councillor and Civic Society member Bill Murphy, who lives in Trealaw said: "I believe it is very fitting that Gordon should be remembered in this way.

"Not only did he realise the potential of Tom Jones but he was also a leading light in the careers of many other top stars of the 1960s.

"We should also never forget that he was a very talented songwriter.

"He was never happier than when he was back home in the Rhondda.""

Jo, said that he loved to talk about his early life in the Rhondda and was passionate about the years he spent in the valley.

Jo said: "When he was younger Gordon was very friendly with a boy called Gordon Jones.

"He often spoke about how much he loved to go fishing and bird watching."

Jo, who was a champion high diver as a youngster, was also runner up in a "'Miss South Africa" competition.

She said: "Without my knowledge my mother sent a picture of me to a local newspaper who were running a Miss South Africa competition.

"I went through to the final but lost out to a girl called Adele Kruger who eventually went on to become Miss World."

At just 17-years-old, Jo came to England in search of a modelling career but found ithard to earn a decent living.

She eventually joined the famous Bluebell Dance troupe and moved to Las Vegas to dance at the famous 'Stardust Hotel'.

After a few years, Jo returned to London and her modelling career took off.

Jo was at the height of her career when she met Gordon at a party given by singer Terry Dene.

London born Terry Dene had a 1950s hit with the song "A White Sports Coat.".

"I met Gordon at a 21st birthday party, he arrived with Engelbert Humperdinck, who was still Gerry Dorsey at the time," recalled Jo Mills.

Meanwhile Sonia can recall the time that she and Johnny visited the Mills home when Gerry Dorsey, who later changed his name to Engelbert Humperdinck was living there.

It was Gordon Mills who persuaded Dorsey to change his name to Engelbert Humperdinck which is the name of the German composer famed for his opera "Hansel and Gretel."

Sonia said:"Gerry needed a shirt ironed because he had a gig to perform at so I picked up the iron and did it for him.

"Pat his wife was in hospital having their first baby and he was in a real panic.

"I was only too happy to give a helping hand."

Jo Mills said, "There was just something about Gordon, you just felt he was very sure about his life,

"We were soon engaged and got married in London."

Following their marriage in 1962 Jo saved up and bought him his first piano and together they wrote songs with singer Lou Reed including "It's Not Unusual."

They remained as man and wife for 21 years before they were divorced.

Jo Mills sadly died in 2014.

She said: "I am delighted that the people of the Rhondda have chosen to remember Gordon in this way.

"He loved talking about the valley."

An inscription on Gordon Mills grave stone reads "Though his smile has gone forever and his hand we cannot touch.

"We shall never lose sweet memories of the one we loved so much.

"To the world he was just a part. To us he was the world."

CHAPTER 5

ALTHOUGH Johnny never shared the stage with singer David Alexander they did meet up on a few occasions.

Blackwood born Alexander is much remembered for his hugely popular 1971 song "If I could see the Rhondda One More time."

Born Derek Ebdon he was given the name David Alexander by his manager Byron Godfrey, legal name Raymond William Godfrey, an old teenage friend.

Godfrey and his partner, Raymond John Glastonbury's made a successful London High Court action against singer Tom Jones, who they had discovered and managed.

Both Godfrey and Glastonbury, were also from Blackwood, together known as Myron and Byron in the music business.

Godfrey, along with musical arranger Tony King and singer songwriter/comedian Johnny Caesar produced the EMI single which many call the "Rhondda Anthem".

Johnny Caesar, who hails from South Shields, wrote the words to the popular song in 1968 while sitting in a pal's house in Quakers Yard.

In an interview with Rhondda Leader reporter *Dave Edwards* he said:"I was performing in clubs in the area and I woke up one sunny June day and looked towards the Rhondda and the lyrics and music were written in half an hour.

"I have always had a great romance with the Rhondda I was inspired by the valley's landscape which was littered with pylons and industry."

Mr Caesar, also played the part of Seth Armstrong's sidekick Bill Middleton in the ITV soap "Emmerdale"

In an interview reported in the *Rhondda Leader* in 2009 the South Shields man, who has also written for Tom Jones, had produced a new CD called "Back to the Rhondda" featuring 12 songs about the South Wales Valleys.

The ex-Emmerdale star's album features songs about mining and boxers of Wales among other things.

One of the 64-year-old's songs is an eight-minute description of the Aberfan disaster.

He said:"I was in Aberfan two weeks after it happened and it should never have happened.

"It was horrendous, the power of the thing was incredible,"

He found it hard to write about the events of Aberfan until decades after the disaster itself.

During his time in the area, Johnny made many friends, owing in part to his coming from a mining area himself.

Long time friend, author Bill Richards, of Glynogwr, said: "I don't think Johnny can explain his love of Wales.

"His writing is so typically Welsh it annoys me that he's English sometimes!"

In November 1991, there were fears that David Alexander's singing career, which included such memorable songs such as "Working Man", "Come Home Rhondda Boy" and "My Wales" was over when he was diagnosed with polyps (growths) in his throat.

After surgery and a month of intensive therapy, he recovered and was back singing.

In November 1994, Alexander was rushed into

hospital and diagnosed with cardiomegaly (an enlarged heart).

He was advised by doctors to limit his workload. On the morning of 4 February 1995, he suffered a heart attack and died, he was 66 years of age.

Sonia said:"Johnny admired David and was saddened to hear that he had died. He had a lot of respect for him".

Another singer that Johnny worked with was London born singer Dickie Valentine who became a household name in the 1950s.

In addition to several other Top Ten hit singles Valentine had two chart-toppers on the name in the 1950s UK Singles Chart with "Finger of Suspicion" (1954) and the seasonal "Christmas Alphabet" (1955).

Sonia said:"Dickie was very impressed with John's singing and said he would help him as much as he could.

"It was such a shame that he died so tragically.

"He said that he had an agent called Eddie Jarrett, who had a folk group called "The Seekers" among his clientele and perhaps he could find an opening for John."

"The Seekers" are an Australian folk influenced pop quartet originally formed in Melbourne in 1962.

They were the first Australian pop music group to achieve major chart and sales success in the United Kingdom and the United States.

The Grade Organisation were willing to represent them, and Grade staff agent Eddie Jarrett already had gigs lined up for them.

The song, "I'll Never Find Another You" was recorded at Abbey Road studios and became the first song by an Australian group to reach number one in the UK.

Dickie Valentine told Jarrett how impressed he was with Johnny which prompted the agent to send him a letter inviting him up to London to have a chat.

Sonia said:"Eddie Jarrett looked after us really well.

"He took Johnny and I to a fabulous restaurant where we enjoyed a lovely meal.

"It was while we were there I noticed a chap who kept staring towards us.

"He looked familiar but I just couldn't place him.I knew I had seen somewhere but I couldn't think where.

"He just kept looking over toward us and to be honest I was beginning to think he mistakenly thought John was Tom Jones.

"I later discovered that the chap keeping an eye on us was none other than well known magician and television personality David Nixon."

At the height of his career, Nixon, who died in 1978, was the best-known magician in the UK.

The London born entertainer appeared regularly on TV whilst his other claim to fame was being Basil Brush's first partner.

Sonia said:"When we eventually returned to his office Eddie took a pile of records out of a drawer and asked John if he knew any of them to which he replied that he knew all of them.

"Eddie then asked if John would record one or two of them in a bid to break into the American market before recording a song of his own.

"John shook his head flatly refused the request which didn't surprise me at all but he did give

Eddie the name of a singer called Tim Jones who might do it".

Sadly while travelling to a gig in the Double Diamond club in Caerphilly the Dickie Valentine was killed outright in a car crash on a single lane bridge at Glangrwyney, near Crickhowell, on 6 May 1971, at the age of 41.

Pianist Sidney Boatman and drummer Dave Pearson, aged 42 also died.

Sonia said:"John was shocked and saddened when he heard that Dickie had died. He admired him a lot."

In the 1970s the Double Diamond club was a hugely popular venue attracting some of the best known names in show business,

The acts that appeared on stage there included Lionel Blair, Dave Allen, Eartha Kitt, Caerphilly born Tommy Cooper, along with Chuck Berry, Jerry Lee Lewis, Pat Boone and Roy Orbison.

In 1981 American singing start Johnny Cash performed there

The club gave fans the chance to see major British and American acts and many will remember the starry lights in the ceiling made to look like the Caerphilly sky.

Because of financial difficulties the once hugely popular club closed in April 1984.

Johnny Bennett was also one of the guest entertainers at Bernard Manning's Embassy Club in Manchester.

Bernard Manning was an English comedian and night club owner who became famous on British television in the 1970s appearing on shows including "The Comedians" in which one of Johnny's pals Bryn Phillips regularly appeared, and "The Wheeltappers and Shunters Social Club".

The controversy surrounding his acts meant that Manning was rarely seen on television in the later part of his career but he continued to perform in pubs and clubs until his death in 2007 at the age of 67.

Sonia said;"A strange thing happened when Johnny performed at the Embassy.

"John was getting a great ovation when Bernard asked for the volume down.

"That was something he never did and Johnny and I could never figure out why he made that decision."

The comedian made several appearances in valley clubs including the Trealaw Social better known as "The Rez" where after his act had finished the regulars had to push his car because the battery had gone flat.

Sonia said:"One of Johnny's favourite venues was the Band Club in Nantymoel.

"John loved playing there.They were his kind of people."

The Band Club, located in Pricetown, along with the Top Club and the Blaenogwr Hotel were among the watering holes for the locals during the 1960s.

The trip for a performance at the Band Club was a short one for Johnny with the village of Nantymoel being just the other side of the Bwlch Mountain.

Nantymoel resident Julie Bennett said:"My mam and dad were the steward and stewardess and became very good friends with Johnny and Sonia.

"When they ran the Band Club I can remember sitting behind the bar when I was aged thirteen and John was the concert compere on a Saturday night.

"Some years ago we went to see a stage show called the 'Tom Jones Story' and Johnny Bennett was mentioned in the show".

"Tom: A Story of Tom Jones" was premiered in the music legend's home town of Pontypridd on St David's Day 2014.

It also happened to be 49 years to the day that his massive hit, "It's Not Unusual", topped the charts.

However Sir Tom was unable to attend the show..

When Johnny Bennett finished his act at the Band Club he was always sure to get a welcome from an Italian owned shop in Treorchy.

Sonia said:"Whenever John needed to travel through Treorchy after finishing his act the Carpaninis café in Bute Street would always stay open for him.

"The café owners Ernie and Luisa were a lovely couple and were always pleased to see us.

They were convinced that because of his looks John was Italian".

Born in Bardi, Italy Louisa opened the cafe in Bute Street with her husband Ernesto in 1947.

Sonia said:"They would talk a lot to about Bardi in Italy where the family were from and although John would nod his head knowingly he didn't have a clue what Ernie and Luisa were talking about.

"We always enjoyed going there. We always had a warm welcome.".

In the 1960s *The South Wales Echo* ran a story with the headline "Contract for 'New Tom' after the show"

The report said that a new "Tom Jones" singer from Tonypandy was acclaimed by a capacity audience at The Lord Mayor's matinee at the New Theatre in Cardiff.

It said:"After the show Johnny, an extremely versatile singer, was offered a recording contract by EMI agents from London who went to the show just to see him.

"With his backing group "The Triangles" Johnny seemed reminiscent of Tom Jones as he swung his way through both ballad and beat numbers".

The contract never happened however denying
Johnny Bennett another opportunity a step up in
his singing career.

During his singing years Johnny made many
friends.

 One in particular was a DJ named John Morris he
met in a club in Tonyrefail.

Sonia said:"The DJ's mother owned a caravan in
Borth and we had many free holidays there.

"She was really good to us."

Sadly Mr Morris died in February 2019 at the age
of 72.

Many Tributes were paid to John Morris. Mr
Morris, who had moved in famous musical circles
during the '60s and '70s, had been suffering from
diabetes and other health complications and had
several extended stays in hospital.

Well-known as a DJ, he toured the country with
Emperor Rosko in the 1970s and 1980s after
helping launch the idea of the Radio 1 roadshow.

Mr Morris became a DJ after returning to
Ceredigion in the 1970s from spending time in
London where he made friends with the great and
good of the British music scene.

He brought the roadshow to Aberystwyth every year and has worked with famous DJs including Dave Lee Travis, Noel Edmonds and Mike Reid. His show was known as Spot on Disco, with Mr Morris himself becoming to be known as "John Spot-on".

Ray Lovegrove, a roadie for the Kinks in the 1960s, said Mr Morris was a "larger than life character" who "will be dearly missed".

"He and I had many escapades in the music biz and kept in touch until turn of the early 2000s," he said in an online tribute.

"He spent a great deal of time with "The Who" and throughout his time helped many a struggling band.

"He even took Jimi Hendrix to Aberystwyth and came with me when Jimi and I visited the Aberfan disaster site.

 "I will always remember him as a generous guy."

Sonia also recalled that Johnnie used to visit a voice trainer in London.

"He had decided to use a voice trainer and also had some professional pictures taken but it never really came to anything.

"Performing in valley clubs and other venues in South Wales was definitely his bread and butter".

CHAPTER 6

JOHNNY also always looked forward to performing at the White Wheat night club in Maesteg.

The White Wheat club, which was formerly a cinema, was a hugely popular venue where such top acts as "The Fortunes", "Showaddywaddy" and "The Nolans" performed.

Sonia said:"The White Wheat was owned by Clem Williams and what a character he turned out to be.

"There was a lovely restaurant there and we never missed having a meal.

"After doing a late night show we would all go upstairs to have a meal at the restaurant and Clem always footed the bill.

"Talk about singing for your supper.

"Clem would sometimes stick pins into a doll which always used to amuse John.

"He was fascinated by it.

"He used to have a laugh and say that we had all better watch out because Clem was up to some Black Magic.

"We always had a warm welcome and loved going there.

"They were the sort of occasions you never forget".

One of Johnny's greatest fans was Merthyr born boxer Howard Winstone MBE.

Howard, who sadly died in 2000, enjoyed a hugely successful career in the boxing ring during which he won the World Featherweight title in 1965.

Sonia said:"If Howard knew Johnny was performing anywhere near Merthyr he would make sure he would be there.

"They both enjoyed singing 'Keep on Running' it was their theme song.

"John always had a love of boxing .

"They were good pals and had a lot of fun together."

"Keep on Running" is a song written and originally recorded by Jackie Edwards.

The song became a number one hit in the UK when recorded by The Spencer Davis Group.

 Spencer Davis is a Welsh musician and multi-instrumentalist, and the founder of the 1960s beat band The Spencer Davis Group.

"Davies" is pronounced "Davis" in Wales, but would be misread as "Davees" in the US, so professionally he dropped the E from the spelling to avoid confusion.

In the 1970s Johnny was still being kept busy performing in Rhondda clubs.

He performed on stage in Charmonds in Porth and the Maerdy Hall.

His act was also in demand outside the valley.

He performed regularly at Llanelli Rugby Club and the Dockers Club.

Sonia said:"John was on stage at Charmonds in Porth every Friday night.

"He was always given a brilliant reception there.

"The chap that ran it used to call John ' Body and Soul'.

"He knew John would get a great reception whenever he performed there."

The Ely Miners Welfare Hall was. another venue where Johnny was popular with audiences.

Another one of John's favourite venues was Maerdy Hall, which was demolished in 2009.

The Hall was once a precious part of the community and a hot bed of political activity.

Built in 1905 on land given to the workmen of the

collieries in Maerdy by landlords, the hall has something of a chequered history.

But in the 21st century it is a sad, abandoned relic of Maerdy's once great past.

This last outpost of the Rhondda Fach's proud past is to have another reminder of coal's rich legacy taken away.

There are mixed feelings in the village about the prospect of losing probably its last icon to the era of the mines.

Mike Richards a former trustee of the building and was the last chairman of the

NUM's Mardy lodge told the *Rhondda Leader* that he had a mixed feeling about it and that in its present state it had to come down.

"It has served the community over the years, it has educated people and it has given people lots of pleasure and enjoyment, as most institutes have.

"It has always been the focal point. Not only is it a big building in stature, it has educated people in its library, the stage has held "Gymanfa Ganu" and concerts, bands used to play there.

"It has all gone on in Maerdy Hall.

"Having said that, it is a shame but all good things come to an end. At one time every room in that building was used."

Former miner Ken Thomas, 73, said then:"If they had money they could do it up. I didn't know this was going to happen.

"I should think they could have kept it open and used it for something else."

Wynford Evans, 48, said, "I remember the hall when it was thriving in the '60s and '70s.

"When the pit shut, it became less used and therefore more difficult to run.

"Most people will be sad to see it gone, but it has been closed for a few years now and it has to come down because it is becoming a danger."

The decision to demolish the old building came after a survey among villagers by Rhondda Cynon Taf County Borough Council.

"What became clear was that the vast majority of people felt that the ongoing presence of this large derelict building represented a barrier to the future regeneration of the village," said Ros Davis, Maerdy Communities First Coordinator.

Councillor Robert Bevan, cabinet member for

economic regeneration, said then:"The building's proud history will not be forgotten."

Johnny also sang at the Llwyncelyn Arms in Porth at a time when it was going into decline.

Sonia said:"The owner was always very grateful because when John started performing there business began to pick up.

"There was always a full house when they had singalongs".

In June 1971 John made a big step in his singing career when he became a member of Equity.

Equity, formerly officially titled the British Actors' Equity Association (although Equity was always its common name), is the trade union for theatre directors,fight directors, choreographers, set designers, costume designers, lighting designers, actors, stage managers, models and performers in the United Kingdom.

It was formed in 1929 by a group of West End performers and, in 1967, it incorporated the Variety Artistes' Federation.

The late 1970s and early 1980s also saw the beginning of the decline in Rhondda Workingmen's clubs.

Although Johnny was getting less and less busy with his singing bookings he was still enjoying life to the full.

He had performed at Brizenorton the RAF base in Oxford, did a gig at Butlins in Minehead.

He also appeared on a Welsh language TV show.

Sonia said:"Club was slowly beginning to change in the Rhondda during the late1970s.

"The menfolk would still enjoy seeing to their allotments and looking after their homing pigeons.

"However there were more or less only dedicated members enjoying their nights out in the drinking clubs.

"And the days when you could take a couple of sandwiches and other food to a club concert on a Saturday night were becoming less and less."

John worked with some very talented performers over the years including Johnny Cantrell, Stella King, Karl Harris and Mike Sherlock.

Sonia said:"Although they never had the chance to make it big in show business they were hugely popular whenever they performed in the valleys.

"John was still having his regular bookings but he was also kept busy with another one of his passions.

"He had got involved in the gold trade in London and loved every minute of it.

"He enjoyed making his trips to Petticoat Lane while wheeling and dealing in London.

"John also owned horses which was something he loved.

."He also had a goat he called Winnie who would always make a big fuss of him whenever he got back from a gig.

"Johnny also had a great passion for boxing and when he was younger he did have a few bouts but after one fight against a young boxer called Warren Kendall Johnny decided to hang up his boxing gloves for good.

Warren Kendall from Tonyrefail was a professional boxer who was active between 1936 and 1949

He boxed at flyweight; bantamweight; featherweight; lightweight; welterweight and took part in 116 professional contests.

Sonia said:"John came off worse for wear after his fight with Warren and when he arrived battered and bruised his mother Jesse put a quick stop to his budding boxing career."

John Jones, the former Chairman of the Welsh Ex Boxers Association said Johnny was highly thought of by the members.

Mr Jones said:"Johnny loved his boxing and was always given a great welcome whenever he attended events."

In 2009 former world boxing champion and a pal of Johnny's Howard Winstone became only the second UK fighter to be inducted into the World Boxing Council's (WBC) Hall of Fame.

Howard Winstone Jnr and association secretary Don James were presented with a medallion and certificate of induction in Winstone's honour at the annual Welsh Ex-Boxers' Association convention.

The boxer, from Merthyr Tydfil, got the posthumous accolade 41 years after he was crowned WBC Featherweight Champion.

Following a hugely successful career in the ring the popular boxer briefly ran a cafe in Merthyr, and then a public house in Aberdare, neither venture proving successful.

Always a popular at boxing reunions and a frequent visitor to the Rhondda, Winstone could not help wistfully comparing the ring earnings of today's top fighters with his own modest pay.

He was constantly dogged by ill health and money problems.

Sadly Howard died in September 2000 aged 61.

John Jones, who was a member of the Fernhill Amateur Boxing Club when it was based in the Palace in Tynewydd said:"Johnny was made a member of the Association.

"He was a smashing bloke and I loved being in his company.

"He had a great singing voice and could have gone much further but he just didn't get the breaks"

CHAPTER 7

IN 1965 Mills started working with Gerry Dorsey a
Madras born singer who had been around for a
long time without gaining major success.

Born Arnold George Dorsey the singer had
several hits during the 1960s.

The second youngest of 10 children born to
Mervyn and Olive Dorsey he spent the first eleven
years of his life in Madras, where his father
worked as an engineer.

In 1947, the future crooner moved with his family
to England, where they settled in Leicester.

After leaving school at the age of 15 he did
National Service in Germany.

He began singing in men's clubs, but soon
realized it was a hard way to make a living.

In a TV interview he said that if you were not liked
by workingmen's club audiences you were
quickly told to "Get off".

The singer eventually changed his name to
Engelbert Humperdinck and went on to have big
hits including "Please Release Me" and "The Last
Waltz".

Dorsey's new name was given to him by his manager Gordon Mills the same name as the late 19th century German composer and creator of the opera "Hansel and Gretel".

Without any protest, the singer bought into the idea.

"I had no choice," he later said of his name change.

"I was a starving singer, and someone was giving me a chance to get on in the business."

Sonia said:"Johnny had formed a friendship with the singer when he used the name Gerry Dorsey.

"Whenever he was performing at a venue near the Rhondda he would pay us a visit.

"I always made him welcome. He was always well mannered and polite.

" I found him to be a lovely chap".

Before finding singing fame Gerry Dorsey would be booked for performances in South Wales clubs.

IN 1979 Johnny Bennett, along with 3,000 loyal fans travelled to the Olympia in Paris to see Tom Jones in concert.

It was the Treforest born singer's first concert in Europe since 1976.

The trip was arranged by Tom's Fan Club and Johnny was looking forward to meeting up with Tom again.

He said: "It didn't turn out to be that easy however because when I went back stage I was confronted by a couple of his burly minders who flatly refused my request.

"I wasn't going to give up.

"I scribbled a note and handed it to one of the minders and asked him to take it to Tom.

"He wasn't happy to do it but after going to see Tom he came back and asked to accompany him to Tom's dressing room.

"Tom was pleased to see me and we had some laughs after sharing a few memories.

"We had a lot of catching up to do. It was nice to meet up and chat with him again".

Johnny said that Tom wanted to give him the best seat in the house but he told him he was quite happy with the one he paid for.

"I just wanted to meet up with him again and talk about the old times.

"I didn't want any favours. I wasn't having any of that."

Someone had told Tom that it was Johnny's birthday and when the Treforest born star took to the stage he asked for the spotlight to be turned on Johnny.

Johnny said:"Tom wished me a happy birthday and told the audience that I was the one responsible for teaming him up with Gordon Mills. "That was very special for me. It was a wonderful gesture and something I really appreciated..

"I am thrilled that Tom had made it to the top and I have tremendous respect and admiration for him. "He bought me my first decent sound system and I will never forget that."

While Tom Jones was heading for stardom in the 1960s Johnny was struggling with his sound system.

It was while he was with a pal in Gamlins record shop in Cardiff that John spotted some equipment he could really do with but knew it was out of his price range.

Johnny's pal had Tom Jones' telephone number
and suggested that Johnny give him a call
because he had been very supportive of him.
Johnny shook his head so his pal rang the singer
and asked if he could offer Johnny some financial
help to get a decent sound system.

"Is Johnny there?"asked Tom.

"Yes. He's right beside me."

"Well put him on and let him ask me." said Tom.
But Johnny shook his head. He wasn't going to
ask for any favours.

Tom said;"Tell him to get whatever he needs and
I'll sort it".

Sonia said:"There was another occasion when I
picked up the telephone a voice asked if this was
the home of Johnny Bennett.

"When I said it was the caller asked if John could
come to the phone.

"The next thing I knew he was chatting away to
Tom Jones".

Johnny said:"Tom and I go back a long way and I
had been trying for quite some time to get in
contact with him.

"I knew that he was at the Pop Factory in Porth recently and I tried to get in touch with him there but failed.'

The Pop Factory was a converted soft drinks factory, formerly belonging to the "Welsh Hills" brand (which later became Corona).

The pop factory was situated in the Thomas and Evans building.

Thomas and Evans, who are both buried in the Rhondda, also owned Bronwydd House and Porth Park.

The Pop Factory was officially opened by Tom Jones in 2000, by smashing a bottle of Dandelion and Burdock against its walls.

As well as hosting such names as Pontypridd legend Tom, Victoria Beckham, Stereophonics Cerys Mattthews and Manic Street Preachers.

The Pop Factory also started the careers of others including Gethin Jones, and the Rhondda's very own Steve Jones.

Johnny said:"I was told Tom was on a visit back home so a pal of mine managed to get his security people to hand him a letter with my telephone number on it.

"It was lovely to talk to Tom again.

" The strange thing is that the last time I spoke to him was when I went to Paris also for my birthday to see him perform he invited me into his dressing room".

John said he and the singing star had a 25 minute conversation chatting about their families and the old times and that Tom wanted to stay in touch and would contact him again.

Johnny was destined to chat to the star again while celebrating his 69th birthday when he had a surprise telephone call phone from the singer.

A friend of John's named Ian Westgate had been able to contact Tom when he was performing in Cardiff.

"He told Tom that John wasn't in the best of health and he would love to get a telephone call from him.

"Tom did phone John while travelling to perform in Scotland and John was really pleased chat to him again."

Sonia said "When Tom toured Australia in the 1980s John phoned him and asked if he could visit Emrys and Viv.

"He took up the offer and invited them to the show and also stayed at their home."

Not only was Johnny busy performing at the valley's workingmen's clubs but he also had bookings at the Hillside Club and the Meadow Vale clubs in Tonyrefail.

John's brother in law Emrys first met Johnny in 1966 when Ken Griffiths asked if he would play the drums for the singer in the "Innocents Concert Party".

In the Concert Party were Iris Williams who became an international star and Gill Jenkins who later joined Welsh folk group "Y Triban".

Y Triban was formed in Pontypridd in 1968 and the other members were Eiri Thrasher, Caryl Williams and Bob Richards.

Also in the Innocents Concert Party were Griff on the piano, and Clive Davies on guitar along with Malcolm Innocent.

Emrys said:"When the concert party broke up a new group was formed called "The Spades" with Johnny Bennett as soloist.

"It was the start of Johnny's brilliant singing career which saw him gain such popularity in the valley clubs and further afield.

"Shortly after the group was formed John invited me to meet his family and that is when I met and eventually married Vivienne in 1968.

"So I have a lot to be thankful to Johnny for.

"I will never forget the time Johnny picked me up and took me to Treforest to see Tom Jones and his parents.

"Tom drove us to a local club in his Rolls Royce.

"Johnny was in front with Tom and I sat in the back with Tom's father.

"That is something very special which I will never forget.

"I can also recall when we were performing in a club in Swansea and sharing the bill with Ray Ellington and his band."

Ray Ellington's band was part of the renowned "Goon Show" of the 1950s.

The band was also one of the first in the UK to feature the stripped-back guitar / bass / drums / piano format that became the basis of Rock'n'Roll, as well as being one of the first groups in Britain to prominently feature the electric guitar.

Sonia said:"John had a bigger encore than Ray Ellington and the band leader was very impressed with him.

"He wondered why Johnny hadn't made more of an impact in the music business

"There were also occasions when John would go up to London to do some recordings.

"He would usually stay with a friend who was a detective sergeant in the CID.

"One time he did go to the London Palladium to see Tom Jones perform and after the show he spent a lovely hour recalling old times while in his dressing room."

Sonia said:"John also performed in a venue in London and in the audience was Fred Astaire and Ginger Rogers".

Fred Astaire and Ginger Rogers were iconic dance partners who made motion pictures together from 1933 to 1949. They made a total of 10 films, nine of them with RKO Radio.,

Sonia said:"But despite Johnny putting all his efforts into getting his recordings released there always seemed someone preventing this from happening.

"There was one agent called Raymond Ware who told John that he would do everything to "make him a star."

"But it didn't happen.

"He eventually phoned John and said that he was warned to "back off or he would lose his job.

"I'll never forget the time John was performing at the Wolverhampton Football Club and shared a dressing room with an Irish comedian called Frank Carson.

"To be honest John thought he was crackers telling silly jokes but he was another one who was very impressed with Johnny's singing".

Frank Carson was a Northern Irish comedian and actor, best known on television in series such as "The Comedians" and "Tlswas".

Belfast-born Carson whose catchphrase was "It's the way I tell em." died aged 85 in 2012 at his home in Blackpool after battling stomach cancer Sonia also recalled that Tommy Scott used to travel to his gigs in a fan owned by "Bryn the Fish."

Bryn the Fish, whose proper name was Bryn Phillips, was a popular comedian born in Abercynon,

Much in demand at workingmen's, clubs throughout the UK Phillips had a gift of bringing valley humour to the stage.

Originally a fruit, veg and fish salesman, Phillips gained the nickname 'Bryn the Fish' and was fondly known as this by many people in his locality.

After providing the stage support for fellow Welshman Tom Jones, Phillips turned to cabaret for a living and got his big break appearing on "The Comedians" in 1971.

Subsequently his career took off and he became well known for his charity work in Wales and beyond.

Phillips passed away in February 2014 aged 79 after a short battle with cancer.

Sonia said: "Bryn was a brilliant comedian and a lovely man.

"I have fond memories of the times I met him."

Former businessman Ian Weston Westgate remembers the first time he met Johnny Bennett.

"I owned a garage in Penrhiwfer and Johnny popped in to see me because he had problems with his car.

"It was the start of a long and wonderful friendship.

"I introduced Johnny to Petticoat Lane in London and he loved it."

Petticoat Lane is a famous market in the east end of London and a prominent member was renowned businessman Alan Sugar who got his start as a stall holder on the market.

Ian said:"Johnny used to make regular trips up there browsing around the gold market and leather goods among other things.

"He did have a part time job with me for a while. John was a lovely guy and he certainly had the gift of the gab.

"I know I am among many who believe Johnny never fully realized the singing talent he had.

"He could have made it big in show business but there were always blocks put in his way."

Sonia also recalled the time Johnny did a gig at the Townsman Club in Swansea.

The Townsman, the oldest nightclub in Swansea, was forced to close its doors for the final time after 33 years of being a city landmark.

It became one of the best-known venues in South West Wales, helped by its appearance in the cult film "Twin Town".

But it was forced to close for the final time because of increased competition and changes to the licensing laws being blamed for its demise.

Sonia said:"At the Townsman John was on the same bill as a local singer called Bonnie Tyler .

"A London agent was booked to see John through the Cardiff based Joan England agency.

"John was performing downstairs but the agent thought he was upstairs where he watched Bonnie Tyler perform.

"Once he saw the Swansea born singer perform he didn't bother to watch John.

"The rest as they say is history."

Known for her husky voice Bonnie Tyler shot to singing fame with recordings including "Lost in France" and "It's a Heartache".

Ray Ludgrove was another person who thought he might be able to get Johnny a bigger show biz career.

Sonia said:"Ray took John to London on several occasions but nothing ever developed.

"After these visits John would receive lots of parking tickets through the mail.

"It was very worrying because Ray was responsible for them not John.

"We decided to ignore them.

"We never paid any of them and we heard no more about it".

CHAPTER 8

SONIA was always under the impression that people might have thought that John was earning a lot of money through his singing.

Sonia said:"It John couldn't be further from the truth.

Take for instance John had a booking down the Dow Corning Social Club in Barry which was done through my uncle Billy Jones who was on the committee there and his fee for that was just £25."

Sonia can also recall the time when her father handed over a ten bob note (50p) to John and Tommy Scott, later to become Tom Jones, because they just didn't know what to do with themselves.

"Tommy Scott as he was known then visited our house to spend some time with John.

"The pair of them were lounging about kicking their heels.

"They wanted to go to a club somewhere up the valley but they didn't have any money.

"My father could see that they were both bored stiff so he asked them what the problem was.

"John replied that that they were both skint so he handed over ten shillings to get them out of the house.

"Needless to say he never had the money back.

"I always have a laugh when I think about that".

The 1980s was getting less and less bookings for his act.

Club singers were getting less and less in demand but although his bookings were getting not what they used to be it didn't really bother John.

Johnny may have been less busy on the stage but he was still the popular compere at the Pentre Comrades Club (Pentre Legion) for the "Go As You Please" evenings and it was something he really enjoyed.

For many years the club, located at the bottom end of Albert Street was familiarly known as "The Shack".

The club was formed in 1919 in premises in Ystrad before moving to a building in Llewellyn Street, Pentre, in the early 1920s.In the mid-1920s the club moved to Albert Street in Pentre, adjacent to the Royal Field Artillery Club which was known locally as the Shack.

The correct name is the "Comrades of the Great War Club" but not a lot of people referred to it as that.

However Club secretary David Roderick said that in 2008 a decision was made to rename it as the "Pentre Comrades Club".

David Roderick said:"I was vice chairman when Johnny would be the compere on the Sunday night singalongs.

"The singalongs were hugely popular and always drew good crowds.

"Johnnny and resident organist Charles made sure the nights went really well.

"I loved Johnny's voice and I was a great fan.

"I would not just listen to him at the Legion but also other venues where he would be performing.

"I always looked forward to meeting Johnny and Sonia.

"Johnnie really was a first class performer and without doubt could have made a name for himself in show biz but he always seemed to be denied the opportunities."

Sonia said:"John loved his Sunday nights at the Pentre Legion.

"He always looked forward to them.

"I remember on one occasion when comedian Owen Money was performing there and he couldn't understand why there were so many people going into the downstairs lounge.

"Eventually he came downstairs to find out what was going on and I will never forget the look on his face when he could see the room was packed.

"That's how popular John was."

Johnny was contented with his life in Trealaw. His great passion was taking care of his horses while enjoying family life with Sonia and Karl.

"All the family always called John the Boss and he like that."

Johnny also maintained his friendship with Dai Perry, a boyhood pal of Tom Jones who eventually became the singer's minder.

During a 2015 interview with *Digital Spy* Tom Jones recalled an incident in Venezuala in which he had to act fast to stop Dai getting thrown in jail.

He said:" We got in trouble Caracas, Venezuela because the reporters were all over us.

"This was in 1974 and we were in a press conference in a hotel.

"My publicist said to Dai, 'Get Tom through, he's not talking to any of the press, we'll do it at the hotel'.

"One reporter started kicking him in the back of the legs. So he lost it and he smacked him.

"We get to the hotel and the manager said, 'You've got to get this kid out of the country.

"It was late at night but once the court opened in the morning and the reporter files a complaint, they'll lock him up.

"In Latin law you were guilty until proven innocent, so he'd be in there for 30 days until his case comes up."

"So the manager in this Hilton we were staying at said that if we couldn't get him out on an early flight before the court opens, then we'll use the Hilton boat and get him to Barbados.

"But I had to pay his fine.

"I had to pay the judge off so I could get out as they then held me responsible for it.

"When I tried to leave they had taken my passport, so I had to do a deal with them."

"Eventually they managed to get Dai a flight to Miami, before Tom met back up with him in Vegas for his show.

"It proved to be the end of Dai's bodyguard duties and he eventually returned home to Pontypridd".

Sadly Dai Perry died while doing his regular walk on a Pontypridd mountain side.

Sonia said:"Tom and Dai Perry were good pals and we were both saddened to hear of his passing".

Another big part of Johnny's life was travelling to and from London regularly where he was busy dealing in the gold and leather trade.

"While our house used to be busy with people wanting to book John's singing act it was now busy with callers wanting to buy his goods."

But John never got rid of the singing bug.

As the years went by Johnny would readily get up and sing a song if he was relaxing at a pub or club in the valley.

Although John was a heavy smoker he kept himself fit but there was one occasion when he did give Sonia cause for concern.

"We were walking home when John clutched his chest and gave out a gasp.I thought he might have had a slight heart attack.

"Although he didn't want to show it I could see that it frightened him although he did his best to shrug it off.

The 1990s came in and John was still doing his compere stints at Pentre Legion.

It was during one visit to the Pentre based club that something happened which eventually have a major impact on their lives.

Sonia said:"It was while we were driving to the Pentre Legion that John turned to me and asked:'Which way do I turn here.?'

"We had driven to the Legion on umpteen occasions and I just couldn't understand why John had asked for directions.

"I thought it was rather strange but just put it down to be just a bit of forgetfulness and put it to the back of my mind."

Although Sonia didn't realise it then Johnny was in the initial stages of dementia.

But as time went on Johnny was getting more and more forgetful and to make matters worse Sonia's health also began to fail.

Sonia said:"Johnny was a heavy smoker.

"I always told people he smoked for both of us.

"When Johnny used to be perform I would be sitting in a smoke filled concert hall.

"I suppose these days they call it passive smoking.

"My breathing became more and more difficult and I became really ill.

"I was diagnosed as having pulmonary fibrosis in both lungs"

"Eventually I needed oxygen to be able to cope with the illness".

Pulmonary fibrosis is a respiratory disease in which scars are formed in the lung tissues, leading to serious breathing problems.

Meanwhile Johnny was getting more and more confused and eventually he was diagnosed as having vascular dementia.

Vascular dementia is a general term describing problems with reasoning, planning, judgment, memory and other thought processes caused by brain damage from impaired blood flow to your brain.

Sonia said:"It was a really awful time.

"John had led such a full life and it was distressing to see him like this.

"Very often his moods would change quite suddenly and he could get quite hurtful.

"It was like he was taking his anger and frustration out on the people he cared for.

"This just wasn't the man I had married and spent so many wonderful years with.

"John was a gentle person but this cruel disease had changed him.

"I along with Karl and other family members tried to cope as best as we could but because of John's worsening dementia it became a huge problem.

"It really was a tough time for all the family and I was very grateful for the support I received from a lot of people including my close friend Rita Browning.

"John really disliked hospitals.

"I can recall one occasion when I visited him when he was a patient at Ysbyty George Thomas in Treorchy.

"When we arrived at the hospital there was John sat fully dressed with his case packed ready to come home.

"It was sad to see him like that but you couldn't help but smile."

Johnny had become so ill that he was eventually admitted to the Ty Porth Care Home,which was formerly Porth Cottage Hospital.

Sonia said:"He never knew he was in a care home he would often ask me 'Sonia where am I?'

"My reply would be 'You are in hospital John.'

"He used to smile when I told him that.

"John was a patient there for 22 months before this cruel illness finally beat him and he passed away.

"We were all at his bedside when he took his last breath.

"He was the love of my life but knowing that he had enjoyed entertaining so many people it was heart wrenching to see him like this".

Rhondda born amateur boxing referee Tony
Wynne, is one of many who have paid tribute to
Johnny.

He said;"What a performer. So professional.
Johnny had a wonderful voice.

"I listened to him many times all over South
Wales.So much like Tom Jones".

Neil Davies said:"What a great entertainer. Saw
Johnny perform many times up the Tynewydd
Labour during the 1970s and worked with Sonia in
the Casualty Department at Llwynypia hospital".

In his book *Just Help Yourself* Vernon Hopkins,
who was a member of the Senators group and
later the Squires, said:"Two days after Johnny's
death I broke my hip and was hospitalized so I
couldn't attend the funeral.

"Johnny was a gentleman. He was quiet spoken
and always immaculately dressed.

"Always handsome, he had Hollywood charisma.

"He played an important part in Tom Jones
eventual rise to stardom".

Former *Rhondda Leader* reporter Dave Edwards
said:"The last time I met Johnny was when he
was enjoying a pint in the NUM club.

"We had a chat and while we were doing so one of the regulars looked towards Johnny and said:"You are Tony Bennett the singer aren't you?".

"With a smile Johnny replied:"No I am not Tony.I am the other Bennett called Johnny.Tony has got a lot more money than me.

"I interviewed Johnny on several occasions and he had some remarkable stories to tell.

"I have great memories of Johnny.

"He will always be fondly remembered by many people."

Richard Collins wrote a poem dedicated to Johnny Bennett who he described as a valley boy with a gift for making people feel good by simply singing.

He called the poem *Old Johnny B Good.*

"You've all heard of the Jones boy Tom
Who became a superstar find,
But the stable from which our Tom came from
Hosted his friend of yours and mine,
He too is the son of a miner,
Who has seen all the hardships and strife, No friend of Toms could be finer,

*As he helped Tom to earn his new life, Yeah
you're Ok and then,
His eye for new talent is well-known, His ear for
that different voice,
His encouragement has always shown, to help
without favour his choice,
Johnny did the circuit for a living his career a
success for all to see,
But his way is not taking it's giving because he's
Rhondda is Johnny B,
His eyes are a little weaker his hair little bit thin
but his voice hails no finer speaker,
As the young man within him just sings as a
compere he makes it look easy,
Without pausing not being an actor from the good
acts down to the wheezy,
He injects the feel good factor he's backed most
of the time by our Charles,
A musician to grace any stage no matter what
tempo or beat to the bar,
Charles does it for any songs age so thank you
from all of your friends,
For being just as you should and as this
dedication ends I christen you Johnny B Good".*

Johnny Bennett is buried in Trealaw Cemetery and the inscription on his headstone reads "To the world he was one but to us he was the world. "To be born Welsh is not to be born with a silver spoon in your mouth but music in your heart.".

Sonia said:"John may have gone but he has left precious memories.

"He had brought a lot of joy to many people through his lovely singing voice.

"Many people believed that John could have enjoyed a very successful show biz career but it was not to be.

"As long as he could burst into song he was happy.

"I and many other people believe that behind the scenes there were things going on which prevented John's singing career from flourishing.

"John knew it as well but he was never angry, never bitter.

"He loved being an entertainer.

"He always used to say 'I can sing like that.'

"And do you know something?

"He really could."

Printed in Great Britain
by Amazon

40853067R00068